OTHER BOOKS BY MISHA HA BAKA

POETRY

CONFESSIONS OF A LONELY MYSTIC small talk

SHORT STORIES

CONFESSIONS OF A LONELY MYSTIC short talk

ART & HUMOR

TWO WOMEN CONTEMPLATING THE NATURE OF THE UNIVERSE Print Operas BW

TWO WOMEN CONTEMPLATING THE NATURE OF THE UNIVERSE Print Operas

TWO WOMEN, THREE FLAMINGOES AND A POOCH Print Operas

TWO WOMEN, THREE FLAMINGOES AND A POOCH Print Operas BW

TWO MEN CONTEMPLATING THE NATURE OF WOMEN AND THE UNIVERSE

PORTRAITS OF A LONELY MYSTIC

PORTRAITS OF A LONELY MYSTIC IN 3D

PORTRAITS OF A LONELY MYSTIC DELUXE

PORTRAITS OF A LONELY MYSTIC 3D DELUXE

TREE
HOUSE
POND

TREE HOUSE POND

PHOTOS & POEMS

BY

MISHA HA BAKA

TREE HOUSE POND

ISBN-10: 0-9987941-5-5
ISBN-13: 978-0-9987941-5-0

Published by Ha Baka Book

First edition paperback 2017

Dedication

For God

And Country

Photos & Poems

PREFACE

A wooden cottage in the woods, amidst some trees and a pond.

Serenity, spirituality and physical beauty were so overwhelming that I roamed around taking photographs upon photographs. Photographs, however, were not enough. I had to put words to images. I had to speak about it. Being The Lonely Mystic that I am, you were my only recourse. Being a city-boy, I dreamed of nature.

Dreams can come true.

Tree House Pond

Tree House Pond contains forty photographs and forty poems. This version of the book is in black and white. Much of my formative years were spent viewing the world through Taoist glasses. I was a black and white kind-of-guy. My clothes were black and white. My paintings were black and white. My thinking was Yin and Yang. At some point, I went through a spiritual transformation and opened up to colors.

Living in the country is filled with color, well three seasons of the year at least. I chose to combine my Taoist influences and spiritual awakenings into one, hence Double Take – two ways to see one world. It then occurred to me to do the book two ways also: One version just black and white and the other version black and white and color. This is the black and white only version. The second volume of this series will be Tree House Pond: Double Take.

I hope you enjoy my photography. I hope you enjoy my poetry and I hope you enjoy your visit to Tree House Pond.

Misha Ha Baka 2017

A Return To Creation

A return to Creation.
A quantum shift.
An infinitesimal alteration.
A time-space rift.

Beyond and above
Beneath and behind
Beckoned and beseeched
Became and sublime.

Capitulation abated,
Constraints contained.
Constructs elevated.
Contentment sustained.

Once more to continue,
Only seconds away.
Three verses between us
I've enjoyed your stay!

Bland To Blazing

If all I do

Would really be

A clear reflection

Of truly me.

Then I would never have lied,

Or bent the truth,

Stretched my meaning,

Or ravaged my youth.

On prostituted days,

Paid for my worth,

In compensated ways,

Of lackluster mirth.

Of all I know,

And all I say,

It is only to you,

I reveal my way.

What my heart feels

And my mind speaks,

A true reflection

Of my inner geek.

A child of the heavens.

A son of the stars.

A facet of soul.

A spirit in pars.

Oh, come the day.

The instance, the way,

That block be gone,

Oh! Be that may.

Reveal color from form,

Subservience to peace,

Bland to blazing—my Golden Fleece.

PROGNOSTICATORY PREMONITIONS

Beyond the bush.

Beneath the green.

Sometimes

Takes work,

For seen,

To be seen.

Sometimes complex

Is simple

With ease

When all

That's required

Is to see

Forest from tree.

Sometimes the future

Looks up in the air.

Prognosticatory premonitions,

Quite often are rare.

Sometimes it's better,

So late in the day,

To contemplate, *How*

To change ones way?

The dice have been thrown,

The wheels are in spin,

The tickets bought,

All that remains

Is to win!

A Work In Process

A work in process.

How can it be?

Already hundreds
have passed,

And yet so much to
be.

Decay and fall.

Renew and heal.

Surround and
protect.

Emerge and revive.

How odd?

Unexpected flourishing adorns your aged form.

As a bejeweled necklace

Of strewn sea shells amidst a sandless beach.

Heal quickly and strong

Heal sturdy and well

Your majesty, strength, and testament

Is needed and can't soon be replaced.

In the distance,

There is room for growth.

Surrounded By Diversity

Surrounded by diversity.

Distinct,

Determined.

Of similar ilk.

Differentiated only by distance.

Set apart

By time,

Not space.

The illusion

Of

Becoming.

Light, At Last

Frozen, numb

Senseless, dumb

Stifled, shunned

Ridiculed, undone

Belabored, overrun

Denigrated,

Then some.

Retreat, retire

Acquiesce, rewire

Deficient, transpire

Denied, conspired

Destitute, desire

Momentary, fast

Inevitable, passed

Answered, asked

Expectations surpassed

Destiny cast

And

Light, at last!

Magnificence And Fab

Sometimes it comes

From place unseen.

Sideswipes and surprise

Change the scene.

Sometimes what's right

Drags endless night

'Til inspiration shines

Its brightest light.

"Patience," they say,

"It will come, please wait."

To tread water and punt

—An exhausting fate.

I long for the day

When left is right

When down is up

And slight is might.

How dirt first surrounds

The most beauteous bloom

Deliver me, sweet savior

From drudgery and gloom.

When hidden is seen

When unknown is praised

When brilliance is acknowledged

I will be amazed.

Come light and good fortune.

Come love and good cheer

Come wisdom and blessing.

Come close, come near

Change this bleak landscape

This colorless drab

To gold, glittering rainbow

To magnificence and fab!

I Remember When

I remember when,

I was free.

To do and say,

What I may.

To be my way,

As I might.

To go or stay,

Wrong or right.

But now I'm hued,

With colors gone.

Once black was blue

Once new is worn.

Once bright and cheer,

Now bland and drawn.

I long to be,

The me I was.

When me was me,

Before do did does.

Oh, colors bright,

I call upon thee,

To return my youth

My old vitality.

To reveal me more,

So that all can see.

The bright I be,

This be my plea.

My Way

Old, tattered and worn.

Am not at a place

I thought,

I would be

From when

I was born.

They say,

"All is

as should be."

Then who I am,

Is the right me.

There is still

Color enough

To change the day

And marshal my strengths

To do it my way.

Bramble Bush

You'd think,

It would matter.

"Of course,"

You would say:

"It's obvious,"

You chatter:

"Hey,

I would see

It my way."

"If only,

More definition."

"Perhaps

More resolve."

"I know I can do it."

Then I would solve,

All the mystery and confusion,

That lies ahead.

All the fetters and illusions

Finally put to bed.

And yet,

When I arrived at

That distant wall.

Only colors came clearer,

I was still at a stall.

Bramble bush,

Divinity sublime.

Unravel your mysteries,

So I can divine.

Your purpose for me.

What I'm meant to do.

What words to speak?

That would ring true.

Some Mysteries

And then at times...

It is never revealed.

Some mysteries,

you see…

Are always concealed.

Look as you may,

Look as you might,

As far as you see,

Even further than sight.

There is,

Nothing to be seen

The future is,

Hidden in the night.

Only shadows foretell

A coming light.

That will dispel

Confusion,

And deliver

Foresight.

Of Coming Scenes

Barnacled spires of

Incipient liars.

Retracted mires of

Unfulfilled desires.

Denigrated, denounced

Usurped and humiliated.

Deceived, denied,

And nearly asphyxiated.

Quagmired, conspired,

Contained and confined.

Contested, controlled.

Yet mine is still mine.

Distant dreams

Of golden gleams

Beam azure streams

Of coming scenes.

Golden Elixir

What's
out,
Is in.
Other
worlds,
In view.
Once
built,
Remains,
Sustained,
Renewed.
Inner source,
Expands,
Explores,
Refines.
Openings
Reveal—
Plan,
Purpose,
And more.
Light,
Oh, Essence,

Divine,

Sublime.

Golden

Elixir

Towards you

I climb.

Warmth,

Joy,

Clarity,

In chorus,

In song.

Serenade

Your comfort,

Melodious

And strong.

One More Than Me

Another day,

Another way.

"Hi" is "Hey."

"Speak" is "Say."

Rooted and firm,

Amidst all change.

Inner fire

And flame,

Remain the same.

Come flow

That flees.

Come ripple

That rides.

To your love, I cling,

And my time, abides.

When conicals align,

When spheroids adjoin,

When heaven descends

And enters my loins.

I patiently wait,

Firm in stance.

With welcome, I spy

Perhaps, perchance.

A glimmer of thee,

A longing for we.

A wish to be,

One more than me.

A Walk In The Woods

When will up be easy?

And down be done?

Rich be medium,

And health be norm?

New shoes comfortable,

Friends easily found?

Tolls be free,

And peace be sound?

A walk in the woods,

All be gone.

Serenity surrounds,

Equality abounds.

No strife, no effort,

To cross that bridge.

Unless of course,

It is up that hill.

How Nice It Would Be

How nice it would be

If the path was clear

How nice it would be

If I could see

Far into the distance

Its winding bends

Its swirling turns

To gleam its resolve

The sacred to know

All is revealed

With a want to know.

Double Whammy

Double whammy,

Double fool.

Duped by duplicity,

Difficult a school.

Of

Downed and damaged,

Of

Declined and denied,

Of

Delayed and denigrated,

At attempts

All tried.

But

I focus

Not on waters,

But

On

Multicolored trees.

On

Boats to attainment,

On

Paths yet to be.

For

I am at

Onement.

For

I am at

Peace.

And

All that precedes me,

No longer needed—

I now release.

Bright Future Bold

It only takes,

The slightest

Skew.

To change a

Stance,

To alter

A view.

Yet small

Maybe,

A new found

Glance,

How what

You see,

Is worth the

Chance,

To find

New meaning,

Amidst

The old.

Perspective

Changed,

Bright future – bold.

The Hidden Things

I looked within

To seek and find

The hidden things

No longer mine.

I rummaged about

Tossing hither and here,

Not needed bouts

And neglected fears.

Filled to the brim,

No room for more.

Out with the old,

No room to store.

Fresh memories, new love—

Glad tidings, good cheer.

Abundant good fortune—

Come enter right here.

I've done my part,

Worked hard and long.

With patience and persistence,

Never wavered – always strong.

Please do your part.

Refill, renew and revive.

Add bounty to the coffers

And allow me to strive.

New heights, new wisdom

New insight, new light.

Clear vision, bright future

New volumes to write!

Melody Sings Song

A snippet,

A glance,

Minutia,

Perchance.

Not all-important,

Monumental,

Instrumental or

Happenstance.

Casual acquaintance.

Haphazard collide.

Wrong number,

Missed exit,

Yet order abides?

How's possible?

Unexplainable,

Unconnected,

Exists?

In a world filled with order,

How does random persist?

Perhaps distance

Explains

It.

Perspective,

Or view?

Maybe

Chaos is pattern,

Not meaning

Askew.

I'm sure.

From a distance,

From far enough

Up high.

Coincidence

Is planned

Circumstance

And

Meeting you

Will be why.

I've waited a lifetime

Perhaps longer or two,

Before destiny meets waiting

And

Melody sings song.

Nothing For Nothing

Nothing for nothing.

Sometimes is there.

To be without something.

Just to be.

And then it comes,

Whispered winds of colored change.

Undulating ripples cascade,

Bringing welcome change.

YOU SEE WHAT I SEE

You see winter.

I see spring.

You see snowfall.

I see ochre carpets of bronzed leaves.

You see iced reflections of frozen moments caught in time.

I see fluid undulations of ever so slight rippled, cascades of
fleeting serenity.

You see barren skies,

Empty of sign and absent wonder.

I see turquoise heralds of coming joy.

You see eclipsed remnants

Of aged testament to traveling time.

I see mirrored permutations

Of essence projected far beyond the confines of perimeter bound.

You see static stasis

Untouched by change.

I see resilient reserve

Pregnant with expectations

And imminent surmise.

You see what I see is the same.

Only I see what you see,

By a different name.

I Am Blessed

Not all events

Reveal their past.

Not all relationships

Are meant to last.

Not all plans

Unfold as cast.

Not all accomplishments

Mature so fast.

Not all questions have been asked.

Some plans are

Partially revealed.

Some truths are

Often concealed.

Some wounds

Are difficult to heal.

Some decisions are

Difficult to wield.

Some secrets

Will remain sealed.

Eclipsed, the sun.

Cloudless, the sky.

Change of leaves.

Waters flow by.

I am comforted

And caressed

By your warmth,

Your wonder.

I am blessed.

Hidden Ways

It's not as obvious,

It's not as clear.

No matter distance,

Far or near.

The veil is drawn,

Tight and true.

To reveal all within—

Would change

All we knew.

Delayed days,

Hidden ways.

To flow past not yet

And arrive at all set.

One more moment,

One more cycle.

One more excuse

To have to stifle.

Pregnant purpose,

Significance driven.

Outreach sought—

For meaning given.

Like rock within waters,

I will stand my way.

Put full weight forward,

Then have my say.

Too Too

Too hot to handle

Too bright to look,

Too green to eat,

Too done to cook.

Too dense to pass through,

Too tricky a feat,

To escape unscathed,

Too difficult to cheat.

Too, too much,

Too, too many.

To make a difference?

To me, that's plenty!

Too clear to miss.

Too close to ignore.

Too foolish to avoid.

To bright futures and

Right doors!

What Color Your World?

What color your world?

Bleak and bland?

Copied and cloned?

Unique and grand?

What form your stand?

Broken and bent?

Constrained and confined

Useless and spent?

What feel you flow?

Turbulent and torrid?

Absent and denied?

Expostulatory and florid?

What unseen be seen?

Harsh and defined?

Restrictive and contained?

With wonder and sign?

Of worlds, I have seen

Of stands, I have stood

Of feelings, I have felt

I see only your good.

WHAT BEAUTY HIDES

I can't imagine

What beauty hides?

I can't fathom

Such surprise.

Such depth,

Such splendor,

Curtailed

From view.

You abound

In mysteries

Known

But to a few.

Flow By It And Pass

Not all is grandeur

Not even grand.

Not all is wonder

Some, even bland.

Some points—

A way-place.

To pass,

Then bye.

To notice

Beauty

From a corner

Of the eye.

But problems lay

When having stuck

In one place forever.

A perpetual rut.

Like river

Runs through it,

Flow by it and pass,

For life's dull moments,

Were not meant to last.

Distance Or Time?

Distance or time?

Or is it both?

Grand illusion revealed.

Steady you stay

It is I that changes.

And yet it is you

That grows.

Truth is steady

Change doesn't change.

Relationship

Alters perspective

And movement

Perception

Form then substance

Thought then deed.

It Isn't There?

Nestled and

Intertwined.

Discernible amidst

Differentiation.

Obvious upon

Detection.

Hidden

Unless directed.

Diminutive

Until approached.

And you say,

"It isn't there."

Phantom Lake

Phantom lake

Hidden lair

Overgrown

Undergrowth

Upside down

In repair.

Overlooked

Underrated

Often missed

Sometimes dissed

Same old

Same old

Get

The gist?

Turn me over.

Brush the weeds.

Pull the cobwebs.

Do what needs

To be undone

To be, to do

To enter waters

Azure blue.

To sail upon

Life's upstream flow.

To arrive at

All I know.

What Memories Define

What memories define

Times to come.

Expand beyond

Present confines.

Beauty lies in

Past reveries.

Albeit stale

Faded and

Forgotten.

Buttons pushed.

Emotions contained,

Tearful embrace.

See the present

Emerge from

Ripe waters

Flowing to

Future memories

Now

Gone and away

With

New to behold.

Not All Is Beautiful

Not all is beautiful,

Much is plain.

How great the pain

To know

How true

Beauty missed

And opposite gained.

And yet,

Often met

Disdain falls.

Leaving

Inner warmth

Bright—Above all.

SERENITY SOUGHT

Serenity sought!

Languid liquidity

Lavish lucid

Sensuality.

Pristine wafts

Of perfumed

Archetypical

Drifts

Cascade in

Sonorous waves

Of silent,

Motionless,

Undulating,

Redundant

Cacophonies.

And you say,

"S.O.S."

Requiem For A Tree Trunk

Twilight comes.

Not all things last.

What once grew strong,

Now falls quite fast.

Hotels in the sky,

Bridges in the air,

Once joined as one,

No longer a pair.

I mourn for your majesty,

Your stature, your form.

But this moment was destined,

The moment you were born.

Let image be your testament,

Your legacy when long gone,

That you'll be here forever,

Though fallen and torn.

YOUR INNER BEAUTY

There's more to a house,

Then its walls.

What once was short,

Can often grow tall.

Not all that's perfect,

Is perfectly straight.

Sometimes lasting

Requires long wait.

And casual glance

May never reveal

Your inner beauty

Lay hidden and concealed.

Let Come What May

It looks like

Forever

And still won't

Change

Yesterday's gone

Today's the same

Then it comes

Gushing forward

Driven flow

The bridge

Between moments

Comes cross

My way

Bland is colored

Empty if filled

Listless is swollen

Firm is grown

Tomorrow is here

Today of yesterday

I wade in its waters

Let come what may.

Be What You Are

I know you're here.

So many times.

So many confirmations.

It isn't even a question.

Sight unseen.

Sound unheard.

Feelings yet to feel.

Caress' yet to savor.

I see your azure eyes

Strike out from

Your opalescent skin.

Your auburn hair

Waft by

Your reddened lips.

Your black,

Protruding lashes

Shade

Your exuberance within.

Below above.

Sans—

Within without.

Austere

Platitudes—

Exiled,

Removed.

Adrift upon

A shoreless sea.

Alone

Amidst

A myriad of form.

Seeking survival,

Above all else.

See they not

Your waiting arms

And heartfelt smile?

How far is forever?

How close is the Now?

How soon is what isn't?

Forsake your majesty

For cold steel walls?

Renounce your embrace

For wads of cash?

Abundance has changed.

There are now new laws

Written by novices.

Look deep

Spy far

Feel strong

And…

Be what you are!

Sweet God Of Mine!

I know you are there.

You are everywhere.

Hidden in disguise

I just look to the skies.

In fleeting rapture,

A momentary amaze,

Your beneficent grandeur

In infinite ways

Shines bright

Light eternal,

Warms emptiness

Within,

Brings hope to the weary

And courage to begin.

New love, new creations,

Enterprise or design—

I feel your full presence

And read your signs.

They speak to me softly

They tell me you're here.

I need only gaze upwards

And start to revere.

A good

Life you've given,

In health, I live,

A bounty of plenitude

In all that you give.

Wealth, friends and accomplishments,

Love, happiness, and success,

Inspiration and wisdom,

And all the best.

Abundance and beneficence

Shine brightly on me

For me to reveal

And all to see:

Thy golden light,

Thy brilliant shine,

Thy radiant countenance.

Sweet God of mine!

Tree House Pond

A tree.

A house.

A pond.

A lifetime

Of wait

Compressed.

Fashioned into

Precious

By nature's

Long embrace.

Left changeless

Less within.

Quantum expansion

Now seeking

Significant placement

In the field.

Refinement,

Healing,

Rejuvenation,

Rest.

Sleep—a reward,

Solitude—a gift,

Companionship—a dream.

How rich a state

Where all comes true.

Where what you want

Is what you do.

Familiar routes,

Remembered ways,

Just as real

As waking days.

I'll drift upon waters.

Lay face to the sun.

Then shade

Under branches

And when day's done.

Return to my dwelling,

My castle and reprieve.

And remember future memories

I've yet to complete.

TREE HOUSE POND

Index of Poems

About the Author & Photographer

Misha Ha Baka has worn many hats during his professional career. He has penned several other works including Confessions of a Lonely Mystic small talk, Confessions of a Lonely Mystic short talk, the Print Opera series and the illustrated fictional novels series, Portraits of a Lonely Mystic. He holds a BA in English Literature, an MA in Asian Studies and has studied healing and mystic thought in Asia, England, Israel, and the United States. He is an ordained spiritual healer and ordained member of the clergy. He is a fine artist, a graphic artist, a musician, and a composer with dozens of albums of original music including *Passion*, *Miracle*, and *Ancient*.

Additional Books by Misha Ha Baka

www.habakabook.com

Visit www.mishahabaka.com, www.habakabook.com and www.mikeigh.com for more Misha Ha Baka.

MiKeigh Music

Available for purchase at: www.mikeigh.com.

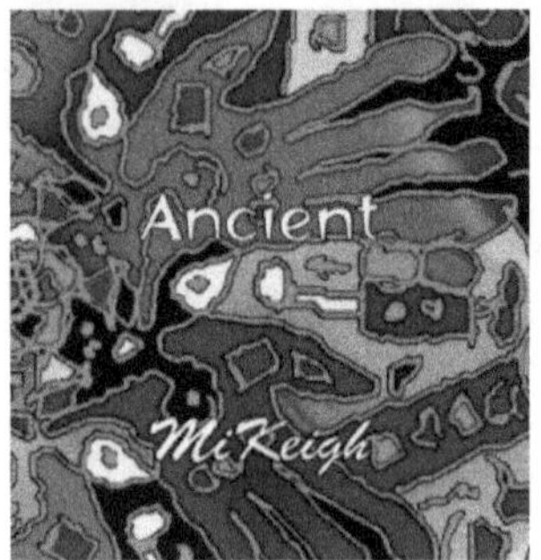

The Lonely Mystic

As Tiny Tyke, the saga begins

"I'm not in a stroller,

This is a High Roller!"

Excerpted from

Portraits of a Lonely Mystic in 3D

For my beloved wherever she may be…

www.ingramcontent.com/pod-product-compliance
Lightning Source LLC
LaVergne TN
LVHW021542080426
835509LV00019B/2782

* 9 7 8 0 9 9 8 7 9 4 1 5 0 *